One True Sentence

Parts of Speech

Kimberly Bredberg, MFA

Sara Evans

ONE TRUE SENTENCE VOLUME A

blackbird & company

EDUCATIONAL PRESS

Visit us at

blackbirdandcompany.com

Explore our full range of Discovery guides:

Hatchling: Reading | Writing | Phonics

Earlybird: Literature & Writing

Literature & Writing

Intro to Composition

Exploring Poetry

Research Science

Research History

Printed in the U.S.A.

First Printing, 2019

ISBN 978-1-947977-05-1

V4 01 Dec 2020

SKU: 20-77051

www.blackbirdandcompany.com

Contents

Introduction 5

Sentence Types 16

Nouns 18

Articles 22

Verbs 26

The Verb "to be" 30

Adjectives 34

Adverbs 38

Pronouns 42

Prepositions 46

Interjections 50

Your Turn.... 52

Introduction

ALL YOU HAVE TO DO IS WRITE ONE TRUE SENTENCE. WRITE THE TRUEST SENTENCE THAT YOU KNOW.

— Ernest Hemingway

"Don't be polite,"
Eve Merriam writes in "How to Eat a Poem."—
"Bite in."
Similarly, Jean L'Anselme writes,
"There are some poets who don't mince their words—
they chew them."

And when it comes to writing exceptional sentences, these statements apply. But in this Era of Information, students are bombarded by millions of hits for every Google search. Over 30 million books have been digitized, and we find it difficult to decelerate, to simply attend to a sentence.

Just as students must ravenously bite a poem to grasp its meaning, they must also chew into sentences. As students slowly probe each inch of crust—relish every particle—they will appreciate the artistic personality of a singular sentence. Contemplating, and in turn constructing sentences, enables students to learn both the mechanics of grammar and syntax, and simultaneously experience the musicality of diction.

Before we begin

Learning to read and write begins at birth. Language is a uniquely human endeavor. Babies respond with coos to our soothing pats and phrases. Next comes the long-anticipated "ma ma" and "da da" and it seems that right on the heals of these adorable utterances are the dreaded "NOs"!

Children are intrinsically equipped to speak, read, and write. Two-year-olds typically speak in phrases (often including the word "more"— *more cookie, more play, more doggy!*), and have a working vocabulary of up to 100 words. At this stage, though they are just becoming able to offer simple statements ("all gone"), simple commands ("eat cookie"), or ask simple questions ("what's that?"), they can respond to very complex instructions: "Take the teddy bear and put it in the toy box."

Four-year-olds have a working vocabulary of 1000 words. Five-year-olds have a working vocabulary in excess of 3000 words. At this age children are using complex grammar in their speech—concrete and abstract nouns, the wide range of pronouns, various forms of verbs. They ask questions. Make statements. Give commands. Five-year-olds delight us with their exclamations as they discover something new about the world they are navigating. On top of all this sentence making, they can sequence ideas, make predictions, compare and contrast, and much, much more.

And how have they accomplished this massive feat? It has been accomplished relationally as they interacted with their family and friends. They've learned about language as they listened to books, conversations, and songs. They've learned about language eavesdropping. They've learned about language as they followed instructions.

Amazing, right?

The study of grammar is to language what the study of anatomy is to science. So imagine what science would be like if all we learned were the rudiments—names of the bones, parts of the cell, structure of the atom—but never experience the wonder of the interaction between the bones and muscles and the fact that this wonder is why animals can move with grace, complexity, and strength. What if our study of a generic animal cell became so important that we never marveled on the fact that within the human body there are 37 trillion cells—about 200 types—all working together in harmony? And what if we, being blinded by the nearly unfathomable abstraction of atomic theory, could not simply marvel in the fact that combinations of distinct atoms make all matter—ALL?

We believe that children, as they read great books, are exposed to diverse information, engage in significant conversation, and write their ideas well, will come to grasp a solid understanding and appreciation of the English language. An appreciation and understanding that moves from a wonderful discovery of the parts and pieces and into the marvel of exceptional communication itself. *One True Sentence: Parts of speech* is a little stepping stone along the way. As students are introduced to the various grammatical roles that words play, they will engage in constructing ideas. And it is this act of constructing that will enable them to discover the wonder of grammar and to master the rules.

For the Teacher

Learning to write well requires tools, skills-based tools. And these tools are acquired as students actually engage in constructing their ideas with pencil on paper. *One True Sentence: Parts of Speech* is an opportunity for students to learn about grammar and gain skills as they construct original ideas.

Sentences are the building blocks of writing. Each week, grammar topics are introduced or reviewed through a controlled example that demonstrates a grammatical pattern. These examples will enable students to actively engage with sentence structure — capitalization, punctuation, grammatical patterns, and syntax.

Over the course of 25 weeks, students will craft more than 200 sentences as they construct with words — the building blocks of ideas.

By *studying* grammar, we become better writers and readers. But when we actually *construct* grammar, writing our ideas rather than learning rules, deconstructing, and diagramming sentences, we become more equipped to communicate well.

Keep the following in mind as you mentor your student through this material:

Use a Dictionary

As you guide your students through this guide, it is useful to have a dictionary nearby.

Depending on its relationship to other words in a sentence, a word may be playing a different grammatical role:

Laugh as a **verb**:

He couldn't stop **laughing** at the clown.

Laugh as a **noun**:

Mother let out a **laugh** when her son told the knock-knock joke.

Laugh as an **adjective**:

The **laughing** baby crawled toward the purring cat.

And this fact should not ever be daunting, but rather a marvelous wonder!

Think Shakespeare

There is no doubt in my mind that he did NOT feel paralyzed by grammar. He once wrote, "Words, words, words!" Then, I imagine he smiled and picked up his pen and wrote his ideas. Isn't that marvelous!

Types and Parts of the Sentence

Week 1 of the journey will introduce the concept of the sentence — the quintessential unit of all real writing. Sentences communicate ideas. Each sentence, be it a statement, a command, a question, or an exclamation, has two parts — the subject and the predicate. This concept is best mastered as students construct ideas.

Example:

If your student writes:

Then the purring kitten.

This is a fragment, a sentence missing the "predicate", a sentence without a verb. In this case, you can ask, "What is the kitten doing?" This will lead to a re-write such as:

Then the purring kitten jumped.

If your student writes:

Running fast.

This too is a fragment, but this time the sentence is missing the "subject", a sentence without a noun. In this case, you can ask, "Who is running fast?" This will lead to a re-write such as:

The leopard is running fast.

The **SUBJECT** is the pronoun, noun, or noun phrase that performs the action of the verb.

The **PREDICATE** is the action and all the attributes of the action.

Example:

The cheerful child climbed quickly to the top of the slide.

The subject is: ***The cheerful child***

The predicate is: ***climbed quickly to the top of the slide***

Grammar Exercises

During weeks 2 through 25 students will explore grammar and style as they craft silly and savvy sentences. In addition to practicing the four types of sentences, they will be introduced to the role of the parts of speech: nouns, verbs, articles, pronouns, adjectives, adverbs, interjections, conjunctions, and prepositions.

Because parts of speech don't exist in isolation, subjects and verbs are often built in phrases ("the silly giraffe", "quietly ran away"), learning to construct grammar enables students to move quickly toward being able to communicate their ideas effortlessly.

All instructions are directed toward the student in the lesson. Each week, as students use words from their deck, or words of their own, they will quickly move toward writing sentences that start with a capital and end with a mark, but more importantly, are delightfully entertaining.

More About Nouns and Verbs

Let's Talk Nouns.

Abstract Nouns *are ideas, concepts, feelings, states, and emotions.*

These words represent things that can't be experienced through the five senses — you can't see it, smell it, touch it, or taste it.

Sometimes abstract nouns can be tricky. Take the word "family" as an example.

In some cases this is a concrete noun:

*My **family** traveled to Idaho to visit Grandma.*

And in some cases it is an abstract noun:

*She longed to experience **family**, especially when the house was quiet at night.*

Following is a list of abstract nouns to expand your student's **Parts of Speech Deck**:

ability	adoration	artistry	bravery	clarity
comfort	courage	dedication	dreams	envy
evil	fear	friendship	happiness	hate
hope	humor	idea	kindness	liberty
love	loyalty	luck	luxury	pain
patience	self-control	skill	sleep	warmth
wisdom	wit	worry		

Concrete Nouns *are set in stone.*

These words represent something that can be experienced through the five senses—you can see it, smell it, touch it, taste it.

yardstick	egg	pencil	sponge	Paris
island	mother	key	ostrich	New York
sister	Los Angeles			

Let's Talk Verbs

All **Regular Verbs** have a form called the "infinitive". The infinitive form is the **root** verb with the word **to** added.

Root: *shrink*   Infinitive: ***to shrink***

English has three simple verb tenses: present, past, and future.

Example:

Infinitive:	***to shrink***
Present tense:	***shrink*** ***shrinks*** ***shrinking***
Past tense:	***shrank*** ***shrunk***
Future tense:	***(will) shrink*** ***(will be, will have been) shrinking*** ***(will have) shrunk***

Get Started

Week 1: **Sentence Types**

All sentences communicate an idea through an object and an action. You will know where a sentence begins and where it ends by its initial capital letter and ending punctuation mark depending upon the type of idea being conveyed.

There are four types of sentences:

1. Statement   2. Question   3. Exclamation   4. Command

▷ **DAY 1**

A **statement** is the most common type of sentence.
The fancy name for a statement is: **declarative sentence**.

Examples

There are four books on the kitchen table.
The books are sitting in a puddle of soup.
My sister is rushing for a roll of paper towels.

Add 2 more statements telling what happens next.

1. _____

2. _____

▷ **DAY 2**

A **question** is a sentence that asks something.
The fancy name for a question is: **interrogative sentence**.

Examples

I wonder why there is an enormous hole in my backyard lawn?
Was the hole there yesterday?
Who dug that hole?

Add 2 more questions you want to ask about this mystery.

1. _____

2. _____

Week 1: **Sentence Types**

▷ **DAY 3**

> An **exclamation** is a sentence that expresses excitement.
> The fancy name for an exclamation is: **exclamatory sentence**.

Example

We won!
What a beautiful day!
That is an enormous whale!
It is extremely dangerous to stand so near the falls!

Add 2 more exclamations telling what happens next.

1. _____

2. _____

▷

DAY 4

> A **command** is a bossy sentence.
> The fancy name for a command is: **imperative sentence**.

Example

Bend over and touch your toes.
Stand up and lift your arms.
Squeeze your fists tight.

Add 2 more commands telling what happens next.

1. _____

2. _____

Week 2: **Nouns**

Nouns are words used to describe a person, place, thing or idea.
Nouns make up the subject of a sentence.

There are two types of nouns:

1. *Concrete* — nouns you can see, hear, taste, smell, and/or touch.
Dog, house, fruit, sky, teacher, book, are examples of **concrete** nouns.

2. *Abstract* — nouns that describe ideas, concepts, or emotions and
cannot be understood using the five senses.
Luck, joy, truth, lie, friendship, fear, are examples of **abstract** nouns.

For each of the following:
1. Read the example sentence aloud, taking note of the underlined words.
2. Read the questions and circle the correct answers.
3. Complete the sentences by filling in the blanks.
   Use your word cards or imagination and follow the hints given below the blank spaces.

▷ **EXAMPLE #1 »**

The dog and the skillet went up the trail.

What type of nouns are underlined?.. **Abstract   Concrete**

What type of sentence is this? .... **Statement   Command   Question   Exclamation**

YOUR TURN »

a) *The _____ and the _____ jumped over the _____ .*
         Concrete Noun   Concrete Noun   What did they jump over?

b) *The _____ and the _____ ran around the _____ .*
         Concrete Noun   Concrete Noun   What did they run around?

▷ **EXAMPLE #2 »**

The gift he gave brought me joy and delight.

What type of nouns are underlined?.. **Abstract   Concrete**

What type of sentence is this? .... **Statement   Command   Question   Exclamation**

YOUR TURN »

a) *The _____ from the store made him feel _____ and _____ .*
         Concrete Noun   Abstract Noun   Abstract Noun

b) *The _____ she borrowed left her with _____ and _____ .*
         Concrete Noun   Abstract Noun   Abstract Noun

Week 2: **Nouns** (continued)

> Following the format of the previous sentences, create your own sentences using words from your word deck and ideas of your own.

▷ **DAY 1**
Craft a sentence similar to example #1.

1. _____

Craft a sentence similar to example #2.

2. _____

▷ **DAY 2**
Craft a sentence similar to example #1.

3. _____

Craft a sentence similar to example #2.

4. _____

▷ **DAY 3**
Craft a sentence similar to example #1.

5. _____

Craft a sentence similar to example #2.

6. _____

▷ **DAY 4**
Craft a sentence similar to example #1.

7. _____

Craft a sentence similar to example #2.

8. _____

Week 3: **Nouns** (continued)

Nouns are words used to describe a person, place, thing, or idea.
Nouns make up the subject of a sentence.

There are two types of nouns:

1. *Concrete* — nouns you can see, hear, taste, smell, and/or touch.
Dog, house, fruit, sky, teacher, book, are examples of *concrete* nouns.

2. *Abstract* — nouns that describe ideas, concepts, or emotions and
cannot be understood using the five senses.
Luck, joy, truth, lie, friendship, fear, are examples of *abstract* nouns.

For each of the following:
1. Read the example sentence aloud, taking note of the underlined words.
2. Read the questions and circle the correct answers.
3. Complete the sentences by filling in the blanks.
   Use your word cards or imagination and follow the hints given below the blank spaces.

▷ **EXAMPLE #1 »**

The hat is under the glove.

What type of nouns are underlined? . . **Abstract   Concrete**

What type of sentence is this? . . . . **Statement   Command   Question   Exclamation**

YOUR TURN »

a) *The* _____ *is over the* _____ .
          Concrete Noun   Concrete Noun

b) *The* _____ *is faster than the* _____ .
          Concrete Noun   Concrete Noun

▷ **EXAMPLE #2 »**

Is goodness hiding in her heart?

What type of noun is underlined? . . . . **Abstract   Concrete**

What type of sentence is this? . . . . **Statement   Command   Question   Exclamation**

YOUR TURN »

a) *Is* _____ *shining on the* _____ ?
         Abstract Noun   Concrete Noun

b) *Is* _____ *filling up his* _____ ?
         Abstract Noun   Concrete Noun

Week 3: **Nouns** (continued)

Following the format of the previous sentences, create your own sentences using words from your word deck and ideas of your own.

▷ **DAY 1**
Craft a sentence similar to example #1.

1. _____

Craft a sentence similar to example #2.

2. _____

▷ **DAY 2**
Craft a sentence similar to example #1.

3. _____

Craft a sentence similar to example #2.

4. _____

▷ **DAY 3**
Craft a sentence similar to example #1.

5. _____

Craft a sentence similar to example #2.

6. _____

▷ **DAY 4**
Craft a sentence similar to example #1.

7. _____

Craft a sentence similar to example #2.

8. _____

Week 4: **Articles**

The three articles in the English language are: A, An, The.

The **definite** article is **the**. Use **the** when referring to something **specific**, a particular person, place, or thing

The **indefinite** articles are **a** and **an**. Use **a** or **an** when referring to something **general**, or something that is one out of a group.

A is used before words beginning with a **consonant**.
An is used before words beginning with a **vowel**.

For each of the following:
1. Read the example sentence aloud, taking note of the underlined words.
2. Read the questions and circle the correct answers.
3. Complete the sentences by filling in the blanks.
    Use your word cards or imagination and follow the hints given below the blank spaces.

▷ **EXAMPLE #1 »**

Run from the crazy duck!

Which word is the definite article? (circle in the above sentence)

What type of sentence is this? . . . . **Statement   Command   Question   Exclamation**

YOUR TURN »

a) *Run from* _____ _____ _____ .
                Definite Article   *Adjective*   *Concrete Noun*

b) *May I have* _____ _____ _____ ?
                Definite Article   *Adjective*   *Concrete Noun*

▷ **EXAMPLE #2 »**

A fresh apple tastes great.

Which word is the indefinite article? (circle in the above sentence)

What type of sentence is this? . . . . **Statement   Command   Question   Exclamation**

YOUR TURN »

a) _____ _____ _____ _____ *great.*
   Indefinite Article   *Adjective*   *Concrete Noun*   *Verb*

b) _____ _____ _____ _____ *far.*
   Indefinite Article   *Adjective*   *Concrete Noun*   *Verb*

Week 4: **Articles** (continued)

Following the format of the previous sentences, create your own sentences using words from your word deck and ideas of your own.

▷ **DAY 1**
Craft a sentence similar to example #1.

1. _____

Craft a sentence similar to example #2.

2. _____

▷ **DAY 2**
Craft a sentence similar to example #1.

3. _____

Craft a sentence similar to example #2.

4. _____

▷ **DAY 3**
Craft a sentence similar to example #1.

5. _____

Craft a sentence similar to example #2.

6. _____

▷ **DAY 4**
Craft a sentence similar to example #1.

7. _____

Craft a sentence similar to example #2.

8. _____

Week 5: **Articles** (continued)

> The three *articles* in the English language are: A, An, The.
>
> The *definite* article is *the*. Use *the* when referring to something *specific*, a particular person, place, or thing
>
> The *indefinite* articles are *a* and *an*. Use *a* or *an* when referring to something *general*, or something that is one out of a group.
>
> *A* is used before words beginning with a *consonant*.
> *An* is used before words beginning with a *vowel*.

> For each of the following:
> 1. Read the example sentence aloud, taking note of the underlined words.
> 2. Read the questions and circle the correct answers.
> 3. Complete the sentences by filling in the blanks.
>   Use your word cards or imagination and follow the hints given below the blank spaces.

▷ **EXAMPLE #1 »**

Why does an old frog hop?

Which word is the indefinite article? (circle in the above sentence)

What type of sentence is this? . . . . **Statement Command Question Exclamation**

YOUR TURN »

a) *How does* _____ _____ _____ _____ ?
　　　　　　 Indefinite Article　　 *Adjective*　　 *Concrete Noun*　　 *Verb*

b) *When does* _____ _____ _____ _____ ?
　　　　　　 Indefinite Article　　 *Adjective*　　 *Concrete Noun*　　 *Verb*

▷ **EXAMPLE #2 »**

Stop the calico cat from purring.

Which word is the definite article? (circle in the above sentence)

What type of sentence is this? . . . . **Statement Command Question Exclamation**

YOUR TURN »

a) *Stop* _____ _____ _____ *from* _____ .
　　　　 Definite Article　　 *Adjective*　　 *Concrete Noun*　　　　 *Verb*

b) *Keep* _____ _____ _____ *from* _____ .
　　　　 Definite Article　　 *Adjective*　　 *Concrete Noun*　　　　 *Verb*

Week 5: **Articles** (continued)

> Following the format of the previous sentences, create your own sentences using words from your word deck and ideas of your own.

▷ **DAY 1**
Craft a sentence similar to example #1.

1. _____

Craft a sentence similar to example #2.

2. _____

▷ **DAY 2**
Craft a sentence similar to example #1.

3. _____

Craft a sentence similar to example #2.

4. _____

▷ **DAY 3**
Craft a sentence similar to example #1.

5. _____

Craft a sentence similar to example #2.

6. _____

▷ **DAY 4**
Craft a sentence similar to example #1.

7. _____

Craft a sentence similar to example #2.

8. _____

Week 6: **Verbs**

Verbs are used to describe an action, state, or occurrence,
and form the main part of the action of a sentence.

Run, fly, count, listen, cry, help, are examples of *verbs*.

Verbs can indicate when the action happens — in the present or the past.

run/ran   fly/flew   sing/sang etc.

For each of the following:
1. Read the example sentence aloud, taking note of the underlined words.
2. Read the questions and circle the correct answers.
3. Complete the sentences by filling in the blanks.
   Use your word cards or imagination and follow the hints given below the blank spaces.

▷ **EXAMPLE #1 »**

Run, and fold your socks.

Which words are verbs? (circle in the above sentence)

What type of sentence is this? . . . . **Statement   Command   Question   Exclamation**

YOUR TURN »

a) _____ and _____ the _____ .
       Verb   *Verb*   *Concrete Noun*

b) _____ and _____ my _____ .
       Verb   *Verb*   *Concrete Noun*

▷ **EXAMPLE #2 »**

The bird sings.

Which word is the verb? (circle in the above sentence)

What type of sentence is this? . . . . **Statement   Command   Question   Exclamation**

YOUR TURN »

a) The _____ _____ .
          Concrete Noun   *Verb*

b) The _____ _____ .
          Concrete Noun   *Verb*

Week 6: **Verbs** (continued)

> Following the format of the previous sentences, create your own sentences using words from your word deck and ideas of your own.

....

▷ **DAY 1**
Craft a sentence similar to example #1.

1. _____

Craft a sentence similar to example #2.

2. _____

....

▷ **DAY 2**
Craft a sentence similar to example #1.

3. _____

Craft a sentence similar to example #2.

4. _____

....

▷ **DAY 3**
Craft a sentence similar to example #1.

5. _____

Craft a sentence similar to example #2.

6. _____

....

▷ **DAY 4**
Craft a sentence similar to example #1.

7. _____

Craft a sentence similar to example #2.

8. _____

....

Week 7: **Verbs** (continued)

Verbs are used to describe an action, state, or occurrence,
and form the main part of the action of a sentence.

Run, fly, count, listen, cry, help, are examples of *verbs*.

Verbs indicate when the action happens — in the present, past, or future.

run/ran fly/flew sing/sang etc.

For each of the following:
1. Read the example sentence aloud, taking note of the underlined words.
2. Read the questions and circle the correct answers.
3. Complete the sentences by filling in the blanks.
    Use your word cards or imagination and follow the hints given below the blank spaces.

▷ **EXAMPLE #1 »**

Can a basket hop?

Which word is the verb? (circle in the above sentence)

What type of sentence is this? . . . . **Statement   Command   Question   Exclamation**

YOUR TURN »

a) *Can a* _____ _____ ?
           Concrete Noun   Verb

b) *Does a* _____ _____ ?
            Concrete Noun   Verb

▷ **EXAMPLE #2 »**

The orange and the teacup rest.

Which word is the verb? (circle in the above sentence)

What type of sentence is this? . . . . **Statement   Command   Question   Exclamation**

YOUR TURN »

a) *The* _____ *and the* _____ _____ .
          Concrete Noun   Concrete Noun   Verb

b) *The* _____ *and the* _____ _____ .
          Concrete Noun   Concrete Noun   Verb

Week 7: **Verbs** (continued)

> Following the format of the previous sentences, create your own sentences using words from your word deck and ideas of your own.

....

▷ **DAY 1**
Craft a sentence similar to example #1.

1. _____

Craft a sentence similar to example #2.

2. _____

....

▷ **DAY 2**
Craft a sentence similar to example #1.

3. _____

Craft a sentence similar to example #2.

4. _____

....

▷ **DAY 3**
Craft a sentence similar to example #1.

5. _____

Craft a sentence similar to example #2.

6. _____

....

▷ **DAY 4**
Craft a sentence similar to example #1.

7. _____

Craft a sentence similar to example #2.

8. _____

....

Week 8: **The Verb "to be"**

To be means to exist. The various forms of **to be** are linking verbs that help other verbs.

am, is, are, was, were, are forms of **to be**.

In this example: **I am drinking**, the linking verb **am**, helps the main verb, **drinking**.
In this example: **The car was speeding**, the linking verb **was**, helps the main verb, **speeding**.

(This volume will focus on present and past tense, other tenses will be addressed in future volumes)

For each of the following:
1. Read the example sentence aloud, taking note of the underlined words.
2. Read the questions and circle the correct answers.
3. Complete the sentences by filling in the blanks.
   Use your word cards or imagination and follow the hints given below the blank spaces.

▷ **EXAMPLE #1 »**

The clouds are floating over the water.

Which word is a form of "to be"? Which word is the verb it is helping? (circle in the above sentence)

What type of sentence is this? . . . . **Statement   Command   Question   Exclamation**

YOUR TURN »

a) _____ _____ _____ _____ *in* _____ _____ .
   Article   Concrete Noun   To be   Verb   Article   Concrete Noun

b) _____ _____ _____ _____ *with* _____ _____ .
   Article   Concrete Noun   To be   Verb   Article   Concrete Noun

▷ **EXAMPLE #2 »**

The drummer was marching in the parade.

Which word is a form of "to be"? Which word is the verb it is helping? (circle in the above sentence)

What type of sentence is this? . . . . **Statement   Command   Question   Exclamation**

YOUR TURN »

a) _____ _____ _____ _____ *in* _____ _____ .
   Article   Concrete Noun   To be   Verb   Article   Concrete Noun

b) _____ _____ _____ _____ *with* _____ _____ .
   Article   Concrete Noun   To be   Verb   Article   Concrete Noun

Week 8: **The Verb "to be"** (continued)

Following the format of the previous sentences, create your own sentences using words from your word deck and ideas of your own.

▷ **DAY 1**
Craft a sentence similar to example #1.

1.

Craft a sentence similar to example #2.

2.

▷ **DAY 2**
Craft a sentence similar to example #1.

3.

Craft a sentence similar to example #2.

4.

▷ **DAY 3**
Craft a sentence similar to example #1.

5.

Craft a sentence similar to example #2.

6.

▷ **DAY 4**
Craft a sentence similar to example #1.

7.

Craft a sentence similar to example #2.

8.

Week 9: **The Verb "to be"** (continued)

> *To be* means to exist. The various forms of *to be* are linking verbs that help other verbs.
>
> be, am, is, are, was, were, been, being, are forms of *to be*.
>
> In this example: *I am drinking*, the linking verb *am*, helps the main verb, *drinking*.
> In this example: *The car was speeding*, the linking verb *was*, helps the main verb, *speeding*.
>
> *(This volume will focus on present and past tense, other tenses will be addressed in future volumes)*

> For each of the following:
> 1. Read the example sentence aloud, taking note of the underlined words.
> 2. Read the questions and circle the correct answers.
> 3. Complete the sentences by filling in the blanks.
>   Use your word cards or imagination and follow the hints given below the blank spaces.

▷ **EXAMPLE #1 »**

The mouse was running from the broom.

Which word is a form of "to be"? Which word is the verb it is helping? (circle in the above sentence)

What type of sentence is this? . . . . **Statement   Command   Question   Exclamation**

YOUR TURN »

a) _____ _____ _____ _____ *from* _____ _____ .
   Article   *Concrete Noun*   *To be*   *Verb*   *Article*   *Concrete Noun*

b) _____ _____ _____ _____ *with* _____ _____ .
   Article   *Concrete Noun*   *To be*   *Verb*   *Article*   *Concrete Noun*

▷ **EXAMPLE #2 »**

The cake is baked in the kitchen.

Which word is a form of "to be"? Which word is the verb it is helping? (circle in the above sentence)

What type of sentence is this? . . . . **Statement   Command   Question   Exclamation**

YOUR TURN »

a) _____ _____ _____ _____ *in* _____ _____ .
   Article   *Concrete Noun*   *To be*   *Verb*   *Article*   *Concrete Noun*

b) _____ _____ _____ _____ *in* _____ _____ .
   Article   *Concrete Noun*   *To be*   *Verb*   *Article*   *Concrete Noun*

Week 9: **The Verb "to be"** (continued)

Following the format of the previous sentences, create your own sentences using words from your word deck and ideas of your own.

▷ **DAY 1**
Craft a sentence similar to example #1.

1. _____

Craft a sentence similar to example #2.

2. _____

▷ **DAY 2**
Craft a sentence similar to example #1.

3. _____

Craft a sentence similar to example #2.

4. _____

▷ **DAY 3**
Craft a sentence similar to example #1.

5. _____

Craft a sentence similar to example #2.

6. _____

▷ **DAY 4**
Craft a sentence similar to example #1.

7. _____

Craft a sentence similar to example #2.

8. _____

Week 10: **Adjectives**

Adjectives are words or phrases that name attributes to describe or modify nouns.

Loud, hard, blue, fast, furry, funny, are examples of **_adjectives_**.

For each of the following:
  1. Read the example sentence aloud, taking note of the underlined words.
  2. Read the questions and circle the correct answers.
  3. Complete the sentences by filling in the blanks.
    Use your word cards or imagination and follow the hints given below the blank spaces.

▷ **EXAMPLE #1 »**

Can a purple basket fly?

  Which word is the adjective? (circle in the above sentence)

  What type of sentence is this? . . . . **Statement   Command   Question   Exclamation**

YOUR TURN »

a) _Can a_ _____ _____ _swim?_
         Adjective   Concrete Noun

b) _Listen to the_ _____ _____ _sing a song._
              Adjective   Concrete Noun

▷ **EXAMPLE #2 »**

The yellow umbrella belongs to Maria.

  Which word is the adjective? (circle in the above sentence)

  What type of sentence is this? . . . . **Statement   Command   Question   Exclamation**

YOUR TURN »

a) _The_ _____ _____ _is taking a much needed nap._
       Adjective   Concrete Noun

b) _The_ _____ _____ _is driving the car slowly._
       Adjective   Concrete Noun

Week 10: **Adjectives** (continued)

Following the format of the previous sentences, create your own sentences using words from your word deck and ideas of your own.

▷ **DAY 1**
Craft a sentence similar to example #1.

1.

Craft a sentence similar to example #2.

2.

▷ **DAY 2**
Craft a sentence similar to example #1.

3.

Craft a sentence similar to example #2.

4.

▷ **DAY 3**
Craft a sentence similar to example #1.

5.

Craft a sentence similar to example #2.

6.

▷ **DAY 4**
Craft a sentence similar to example #1.

7.

Craft a sentence similar to example #2.

8.

Week 11: **Adjectives** (continued)

Adjectives are words or phrases that name attributes to describe or modify nouns.

Loud, hard, blue, fast, furry, funny, are examples of *adjectives*.

For each of the following:
1. Read the example sentence aloud, taking note of the underlined words.
2. Read the questions and circle the correct answers.
3. Complete the sentences by filling in the blanks.
   Use your word cards or imagination and follow the hints given below the blank spaces.

▷ **EXAMPLE #1 »**

Look at the purple cow telling a story to the little worm.

Which words are the adjectives? (circle in the above sentence)

What type of sentence is this? . . . . **Statement** **Command** **Question** **Exclamation**

YOUR TURN »

a) *Look at the* _____ _____ *throwing a ball*
                    Adjective   Concrete Noun

to the _____ _____ .
          Adjective   Concrete Noun

b) *Think about the* _____ _____ *jumping over*
                       Adjective   Concrete Noun

the _____ _____ .
       Adjective   Concrete Noun

▷ **EXAMPLE #2 »**

Please fold the wool sweater.

Which word is the adjective? (circle in the above sentence)

What type of sentence is this? . . . . **Statement** **Command** **Question** **Exclamation**

YOUR TURN »

a) *Please* _____ *the* _____ _____ .
             Verb   Adjective   Concrete Noun

b) *Don't ever* _____ *the* _____ _____ .
                 Verb   Adjective   Concrete Noun

Week 11: **Adjectives** (continued)

Following the format of the previous sentences, create your own sentences using words from your word deck and ideas of your own.

▷ **DAY 1**
Craft a sentence similar to example #1.

1. _____

Craft a sentence similar to example #2.

2. _____

▷ **DAY 2**
Craft a sentence similar to example #1.

3. _____

Craft a sentence similar to example #2.

4. _____

▷ **DAY 3**
Craft a sentence similar to example #1.

5. _____

Craft a sentence similar to example #2.

6. _____

▷ **DAY 4**
Craft a sentence similar to example #1.

7. _____

Craft a sentence similar to example #2.

8. _____

Week 12: **Adverbs**

> Adverbs are words that modify, qualify, limit, or restrict the meaning of a verb.
>
> Loudly, softly, quickly, slowly, colorfully, happily, are examples of **_adverbs_**.

For each of the following:
1. Read the example sentence aloud, taking note of the underlined words.
2. Read the questions and circle the correct answers.
3. Complete the sentences by filling in the blanks.
   Use your word cards or imagination and follow the hints given below the blank spaces.

▷ **EXAMPLE #1 »**

Will they run quickly from the ferocious lion?

Which word is the adverb? (circle in the above sentence)

What type of sentence is this? . . . . **Statement   Command   Question   Exclamation**

YOUR TURN »

a) _Will_ _____   _____   _____ _after_ _____
   Pronoun   _Verb_   _Adverb_   _Article_

   _____   _____ .
   Adjective   _Concrete Noun_

b) _Will_ _____   _____   _____ _after_ _____
   Pronoun   _Verb_   _Adverb_   _Article_

   _____   _____ .
   Adjective   _Concrete Noun_

▷ **EXAMPLE #2 »**

Please speak kindly with their kitten.

Which word is the adverb? (circle in the above sentence)

What type of sentence is this? . . . . **Statement   Command   Question   Exclamation**

YOUR TURN »

a) _Please_ _____   _____ _with_ _____   _____ .
   Verb   _Adverb_   _Pronoun_   _Concrete Noun_

b) _Please_ _____   _____ _with_ _____   _____ .
   Verb   _Adverb_   _Pronoun_   _Concrete Noun_

Week 12: **Adverbs** (continued)

Following the format of the previous sentences, create your own sentences using words from your word deck and ideas of your own.

▷ **DAY 1**
Craft a sentence similar to example #1.

1. _____

Craft a sentence similar to example #2.

2. _____

▷ **DAY 2**
Craft a sentence similar to example #1.

3. _____

Craft a sentence similar to example #2.

4. _____

▷ **DAY 3**
Craft a sentence similar to example #1.

5. _____

Craft a sentence similar to example #2.

6. _____

▷ **DAY 4**
Craft a sentence similar to example #1.

7. _____

Craft a sentence similar to example #2.

8. _____

Week 13: **Adverbs** (continued)

Adverbs are words that modify, qualify, limit, or restrict the meaning of a verb.

Loudly, softly, quickly, slowly, colorfully, happily, are examples of **adverbs**.

For each of the following:
1. Read the example sentence aloud, taking note of the underlined words.
2. Read the questions and circle the correct answers.
3. Complete the sentences by filling in the blanks.
Use your word cards or imagination and follow the hints given below the blank spaces.

▷ **EXAMPLE #1 »**

Their hope came quickly after the rain.

Which word is the adverb? (circle in the above sentence)

What type of sentence is this? . . . . **Statement   Command   Question   Exclamation**

YOUR TURN »

a) We _____ and _____ _____ after
   Abstract Noun   *Verb*   *Adverb*

_____ _____ .
Article   *Concrete Noun*

b) You _____ _____ _____ before
   Abstract Noun   *Verb*   *Adverb*

_____ _____ .
Article   *Concrete Noun*

▷ **EXAMPLE #2 »**

He screamed loudly when he heard our bell.

Which word is the adverb? (circle in the above sentence)

What type of sentence is this? . . . . **Statement   Command   Question   Exclamation**

YOUR TURN »

a) _____ _____ _____ when he heard my call.
   Pronoun   *Verb*   *Adverb*

b) _____ _____ _____ when they saw her dog.
   Pronoun   *Verb*   *Adverb*

Week 13: **Adverbs** (continued)

Following the format of the previous sentences, create your own sentences using words from your word deck and ideas of your own.

▷ **DAY 1**
Craft a sentence similar to example #1.

1. _____

Craft a sentence similar to example #2.

2. _____

▷ **DAY 2**
Craft a sentence similar to example #1.

3. _____

Craft a sentence similar to example #2.

4. _____

▷ **DAY 3**
Craft a sentence similar to example #1.

5. _____

Craft a sentence similar to example #2.

6. _____

▷ **DAY 4**
Craft a sentence similar to example #1.

7. _____

Craft a sentence similar to example #2.

8. _____

Week 14: **Pronouns**

Pronouns are words that can function independently as a noun.
Pronouns refer to the participants in the action.

I, me, you, he, she, him, her, it, we, us, our, they,
them, his, hers, theirs, ours, are all *pronouns*.

For each of the following:
1. Read the example sentence aloud, taking note of the underlined words.
2. Read the questions and circle the correct answers.
3. Complete the sentences by filling in the blanks.
   Use your word cards or imagination and follow the hints given below the blank spaces.

▷ **EXAMPLE #1 »**

Today they sing.

Which word is the pronoun? (circle in the above sentence)

What type of sentence is this? . . . . **Statement   Command   Question   Exclamation**

YOUR TURN »

a) *Today* _____ _____ .
         Pronoun   *Present tense verb*

b) *Today* _____ _____ .
         Pronoun   *Present tense verb*

▷ **EXAMPLE #2 »**

Yesterday we organized.

Which word is the pronoun? (circle in the above sentence)

What type of sentence is this? . . . . **Statement   Command   Question   Exclamation**

YOUR TURN »

a) *Yesterday* _____ _____ .
            Pronoun   *Past tense verb*

b) *Yesterday* _____ _____ .
            Pronoun   *Past tense verb*

Week 14: **Pronouns** (continued)

> Following the format of the previous sentences, create your own sentences using words from your word deck and ideas of your own.

▷ **DAY 1**
Craft a sentence similar to example #1.

1. _____

Craft a sentence similar to example #2.

2. _____

▷ **DAY 2**
Craft a sentence similar to example #1.

3. _____

Craft a sentence similar to example #2.

4. _____

▷ **DAY 3**
Craft a sentence similar to example #1.

5. _____

Craft a sentence similar to example #2.

6. _____

▷ **DAY 4**
Craft a sentence similar to example #1.

7. _____

Craft a sentence similar to example #2.

8. _____

Week 15: **Pronouns** (continued)

> Pronouns are words that can function independently as a noun.
> Pronouns refer to the participants in the action.
>
> I, me, you, he, she, him, her, it, we, us, our, they,
> them, his, hers, theirs, ours, are all ***pronouns***.

For each of the following:
1. Read the example sentence aloud, taking note of the underlined words.
2. Read the questions and circle the correct answers.
3. Complete the sentences by filling in the blanks.
    Use your word cards or imagination and follow the hints given below the blank spaces.

▷ **EXAMPLE #1 »**

How will they eat after hearing the thunder?

Which word is the pronoun? (circle in the above sentence)

What type of sentence is this? . . . . **Statement   Command   Question   Exclamation**

YOUR TURN »

a) *How will _____ _____ after seeing _____ _____ ?*
          Pronoun   Verb   Article   Concrete Noun

b) *How will _____ _____ after tasting _____ _____ ?*
          Pronoun   Verb   Article   Concrete Noun

▷ **EXAMPLE #2 »**

Please move our bicycle into the airplane.

Which word is the pronoun? (circle in the above sentence)

What type of sentence is this? . . . . **Statement   Command   Question   Exclamation**

YOUR TURN »

a) *Please move _____ _____ into _____ _____ .*
              Pronoun   Concrete Noun   Article   Place (noun)

b) *Please move _____ _____ into _____ _____ .*
              Pronoun   Concrete Noun   Article   Place (noun)

Week 15: **Pronouns** (continued)

> Following the format of the previous sentences, create your own sentences using words from your word deck and ideas of your own.

▷ **DAY 1**
Craft a sentence similar to example #1.

1. _____

Craft a sentence similar to example #2.

2. _____

▷ **DAY 2**
Craft a sentence similar to example #1.

3. _____

Craft a sentence similar to example #2.

4. _____

▷ **DAY 3**
Craft a sentence similar to example #1.

5. _____

Craft a sentence similar to example #2.

6. _____

▷ **DAY 4**
Craft a sentence similar to example #1.

7. _____

Craft a sentence similar to example #2.

8. _____

Week 16: **Prepositions**

Prepositions are words that express relationship between a noun or a
pronoun and some other word or element in the rest of the sentence.
Prepositional phrases begin with a preposition and end with a noun.
All of the words in a prepositional phrase come together to function as an adjective or adverb.

On, in, over, through, by, are examples of ***prepositions***.
On the boat, in time, over the water, by the chef, are examples of ***prepositional phrases***.

For each of the following:
1. Read the example sentence aloud, taking note of the underlined words.
2. Read the questions and circle the correct answers.
3. Complete the sentences by filling in the blanks.
   Use your word cards or imagination and follow the hints given below the blank spaces.

▷ **EXAMPLE #1 »**

All the happiness is under the sea.

Which word is the preposition? (circle in the above sentence) Underline the prepositional phrase.

What type of sentence is this? . . . . **Statement   Command   Question   Exclamation**

YOUR TURN »

a) *All* _____ _____ *is* _____ _____ _____ .
    Article   Abstract Noun   Preposition   Article   Concrete Noun

b) *All* _____ _____ *was* _____ _____ _____ .
    Article   Abstract Noun   Preposition   Article   Concrete Noun

▷ **EXAMPLE #2 »**

Put my salamander in the garden.

Which word is the preposition? (circle in the above sentence) Underline the prepositional phrase.

What type of sentence is this? . . . . **Statement   Command   Question   Exclamation**

YOUR TURN »

a) *Put* _____ _____ _____ _____ _____ .
    Pronoun   Concrete Noun   Preposition   Article   Concrete Noun

b) *Put* _____ _____ _____ _____ _____ .
    Pronoun   Concrete Noun   Preposition   Article   Concrete Noun

Week 16: **Prepositions** (continued)

Following the format of the previous sentences, create your own sentences using words from your word deck and ideas of your own.

▷ **DAY 1**
Craft a sentence similar to example #1.

1. _____

Craft a sentence similar to example #2.

2. _____

▷ **DAY 2**
Craft a sentence similar to example #1.

3. _____

Craft a sentence similar to example #2.

4. _____

▷ **DAY 3**
Craft a sentence similar to example #1.

5. _____

Craft a sentence similar to example #2.

6. _____

▷ **DAY 4**
Craft a sentence similar to example #1.

7. _____

Craft a sentence similar to example #2.

8. _____

Week 17: **Prepositions** (continued)

Prepositions are words that express relationship between a noun or a pronoun and some other word or element in the rest of the sentence. Prepositional phrases begin with a preposition and end with a noun. All of the words in a prepositional phrase come together to function as an adjective or adverb.

On, in, over, through, by, are examples of **_prepositions_**.
On the boat, in time, over the water, by the chef, are examples of **_prepositional phrases_**.

For each of the following:
1. Read the example sentence aloud, taking note of the underlined words.
2. Read the questions and circle the correct answers.
3. Complete the sentences by filling in the blanks.
   Use your word cards or imagination and follow the hints given below the blank spaces.

▷ **EXAMPLE #1 »**

Above the ocean you will find the sky.

Which word is the preposition? (circle in the above sentence) Underline the prepositional phrase.

What type of sentence is this? . . . . **Statement Command Question Exclamation**

YOUR TURN »

a) _____ _____ _____ _____ _will find_ _____ _____ .
   Preposition _Article_ _Concrete Noun_ _Pronoun_ _Article_ _Concrete Noun_

b) _____ _____ _____ _____ _will find_ _____ _____ .
   Preposition _Article_ _Concrete Noun_ _Pronoun_ _Article_ _Concrete Noun_

▷ **EXAMPLE #2 »**

Is their shark still in a swimming pool?

Which word is the preposition? (circle in the above sentence) Underline the prepositional phrase.

What type of sentence is this? . . . . **Statement Command Question Exclamation**

YOUR TURN »

a) _Is_ _____ _____ _still_ _____ _____ _____ ?
   Pronoun _Concrete Noun_ _Preposition_ _Article_ _Concrete Noun_

b) _Is_ _____ _____ _still_ _____ _____ _____ ?
   Pronoun _Concrete Noun_ _Preposition_ _Article_ _Concrete Noun_

Week 17: **Prepositions** (continued)

Following the format of the previous sentences, create your own sentences using words from your word deck and ideas of your own.

▷ **DAY 1**
Craft a sentence similar to example #1.

1. _____

Craft a sentence similar to example #2.

2. _____

▷ **DAY 2**
Craft a sentence similar to example #1.

3. _____

Craft a sentence similar to example #2.

4. _____

▷ **DAY 3**
Craft a sentence similar to example #1.

5. _____

Craft a sentence similar to example #2.

6. _____

▷ **DAY 4**
Craft a sentence similar to example #1.

7. _____

Craft a sentence similar to example #2.

8. _____

Week 18: **Interjections**

Interjections are words that express an abrupt remark,
made especially as an aside or interruption.

Oh, wow, oops, thanks, yikes, are examples of *interjections*.

For each of the following:
1. Read the example sentence aloud, taking note of the underlined words.
2. Read the questions and circle the correct answers.
3. Complete the sentences by filling in the blanks.
    Use your word cards or imagination and follow the hints given below the blank spaces.

▷ **EXAMPLE #1 »**

Wow! That airplane soars!

Which word is the interjection? (circle in the above sentence)

What type of sentence is this? . . . . **Statement   Command   Question   Exclamation**

YOUR TURN »

a) _____ ! _____ _____ _____ !
    Interjection   *Article*   *Concrete Noun*   *Verb*

b) _____ ! _____ _____ _____ !
    Interjection   *Article*   *Concrete Noun*   *Verb*

▷ **EXAMPLE #2 »**

Yikes! Is their shark still in the pool?

Which word is the interjection? (circle in the above sentence)

What type of sentence is this? . . . . **Statement   Command   Question   Exclamation**

YOUR TURN »

a) _____ ! Is _____ _____ *still* _____
    Interjection   *Pronoun*   *Concrete Noun*   *Preposition*

_____ _____ ?
Article   *Concrete Noun*

b) _____ ! Is _____ _____ *still* _____
    Interjection   *Pronoun*   *Concrete Noun*   *Preposition*

_____ _____ ?
Article   *Concrete Noun*

50

Week 18: **Interjections** (continued)

Following the format of the previous sentences, create your own sentences using words from your word deck and ideas of your own.

▷ **DAY 1**
Craft a sentence similar to example #1.

1. _____

Craft a sentence similar to example #2.

2. _____

▷ **DAY 2**
Craft a sentence similar to example #1.

3. _____

Craft a sentence similar to example #2.

4. _____

▷ **DAY 3**
Craft a sentence similar to example #1.

5. _____

Craft a sentence similar to example #2.

6. _____

▷ **DAY 4**
Craft a sentence similar to example #1.

7. _____

Craft a sentence similar to example #2.

8. _____

Week 19: **Construction zone: Your turn...**

Construct 4 sentences each day using the tools you have gleaned.
Be sure to include interesting nouns and verbs.
Add the articles, adjectives, adverbs, and pronouns.
Use words from your deck and ideas of your own.
Look back at the sentence patterns explored in previous weeks for inspiration.

▷ **DAY 1**
Statement:

1. _____

Question:

2. _____

Exclamation:

3. _____

Command:

4. _____

▷ **DAY 2**
Statement:

1. _____

Question:

2. _____

Exclamation:

3. _____

Command:

4. _____

Week 19: **Construction zone: Your turn...** (continued)

▷ **DAY 3**
Statement:

1. _____

Question:

2. _____

Exclamation:

3. _____

Command:

4. _____

▷ **DAY 4**
Statement:

1. _____

Question:

2. _____

Exclamation:

3. _____

Command:

4. _____

Week 20: **Construction zone: Your turn...**

Construct 4 sentences each day using the tools you have gleaned.
Be sure to include interesting nouns and verbs.
Add the articles, adjectives, adverbs, and pronouns.
Use words from your deck and ideas of your own.
Look back at the sentence patterns explored in previous weeks for inspiration.

▷ **DAY 1**
Statement:

1. _____

Question:

2. _____

Exclamation:

3. _____

Command:

4. _____

▷ **DAY 2**
Statement:

1. _____

Question:

2. _____

Exclamation:

3. _____

Command:

4. _____

Week 20: **Construction zone: Your turn...** (continued)

▷ **DAY 3**

Statement:

1. _____

Question:

2. _____

Exclamation:

3. _____

Command:

4. _____

· ·

▷ **DAY 4**

Statement:

1. _____

Question:

2. _____

Exclamation:

3. _____

Command:

4. _____

· ·

Week 21: **Construction zone: Your turn...**

Construct 4 sentences each day using the tools you have gleaned.
Be sure to include interesting nouns and verbs.
Add the articles, adjectives, adverbs, and pronouns.
Use words from your deck and ideas of your own.
Look back at the sentence patterns explored in the previous weeks for inspiration.

▷ **DAY 1**
Statement:

1._____

Question:

2._____

Exclamation:

3._____

Command:

4._____

▷ **DAY 2**
Statement:

1._____

Question:

2._____

Exclamation:

3._____

Command:

4._____

Week 21: **Construction zone: Your turn...** (continued)

▷ **DAY 3**
Statement:

1. _____

Question:

2. _____

Exclamation:

3. _____

Command:

4. _____

▷ **DAY 4**
Statement:

1. _____

Question:

2. _____

Exclamation:

3. _____

Command:

4. _____

Week 22: **Construction zone: Your turn...**

Construct 4 sentences each day using the tools you have gleaned.
Be sure to include interesting nouns and verbs.
Add the articles, adjectives, adverbs, and pronouns.
Use words from your deck and ideas of your own.
Look back at the sentence patterns explored in the previous weeks for inspiration.

▷ **DAY 1**
Statement:

1._____

Question:

2._____

Exclamation:

3._____

Command:

4._____

▷ **DAY 2**
Statement:

1._____

Question:

2._____

Exclamation:

3._____

Command:

4._____

Week 22: **Construction zone: Your turn...** (continued)

▷ **DAY 3**
Statement:

1. _____

Question:

2. _____

Exclamation:

3. _____

Command:

4. _____

··

▷ **DAY 4**
Statement:

1. _____

Question:

2. _____

Exclamation:

3. _____

Command:

4. _____

··

Week 23: **Construction zone: Your turn...**

Construct 4 sentences each day using the tools you have gleaned.
Be sure to include interesting nouns and verbs.
Add the articles, adjectives, adverbs, and pronouns.
Use words from your deck and ideas of your own.
Look back at the sentence patterns explored in the previous weeks for inspiration.

▷ **DAY 1**
Statement:

1. _____

Question:

2. _____

Exclamation:

3. _____

Command:

4. _____

▷ **DAY 2**
Statement:

1. _____

Question:

2. _____

Exclamation:

3. _____

Command:

4. _____

Week 23: **Construction zone: Your turn...** (continued)

▷ **DAY 3**
Statement:

1. _____

Question:

2. _____

Exclamation:

3. _____

Command:

4. _____

▷ **DAY 4**
Statement:

1. _____

Question:

2. _____

Exclamation:

3. _____

Command:

4. _____

Week 24: **Construction zone: Your turn...**

Construct 4 sentences each day using the tools you have gleaned.
Be sure to include interesting nouns and verbs.
Add the articles, adjectives, adverbs, and pronouns.
Use words from your deck and ideas of your own.
Look back at the sentence patterns explored in the previous weeks for inspiration.

▷ **DAY 1**
Statement:

1.

Question:

2.

Exclamation:

3.

Command:

4.

▷ **DAY 2**
Statement:

1.

Question:

2.

Exclamation:

3.

Command:

4.

Week 24: **Construction zone: Your turn...** (continued)

▷ **DAY 3**
Statement:

1. _____

Question:

2. _____

Exclamation:

3. _____

Command:

4. _____

· ·

▷ **DAY 4**
Statement:

1. _____

Question:

2. _____

Exclamation:

3. _____

Command:

4. _____

· ·

Week 25: **Construction zone: Your turn...**

Construct 4 sentences each day using the tools you have gleaned.
Be sure to include interesting nouns and verbs.
Add the articles, adjectives, adverbs, and pronouns.
Use words from your deck and ideas of your own.
Look back at the sentence patterns explored in the previous weeks for inspiration.

▷ **DAY 1**
Statement:

1. _____

Question:

2. _____

Exclamation:

3. _____

Command:

4. _____

▷ **DAY 2**
Statement:

1. _____

Question:

2. _____

Exclamation:

3. _____

Command:

4. _____

Week 25: **Construction zone: Your turn...** (continued)

▷ **DAY 3**
Statement:

1. _____

Question:

2. _____

Exclamation:

3. _____

Command:

4. _____

▷ **DAY 4**
Statement:

1. _____

Question:

2. _____

Exclamation:

3. _____

Command:

4. _____